2381

The best way to read this book is to begin at the beginning and read all the way through.

You'll be amazed at what you'll find out.

Artillery House, Artillery Row

D1299847

WORM'S EYE VIEW

The best way to read this book is to begin at the beginning and read all the way through.

You'll be amazed at what you'll find out.

But if you want to read about one particular thing, such as stick insects or garden ponds, look in the index on page 33.

Kipchak Johnson wrote this book. He is an artist and a bookseller.

Thompson Yardley drew the pictures.

ISBN 0 304 31775 6

First published in 1990 by
Cassell Publishers Limited
Artillery House, Artillery Row
London SW1P 1RT

Printed and bound in Great Britain
by MacLehose & Partners Ltd, Portsmouth

THIS IS A WORM'S EYE VIEW

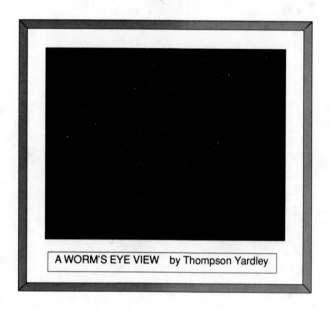

A WORM'S EYE VIEW   by Thompson Yardley

Worms don't have eyes but they
can feel light through their skin.

USE YOUR EYES!..

FIND OUT...how worms find their food!

**FIND OUT...why plants need animals...
and why animals need plants!**

**FIND OUT...how to make a wildlife park...
and make friends with toads!**

ANIMALS MUST GO!

One hundred years ago there were two billion people living on the Earth. Today there are five billion people! And people want a lot of space! They take land away from wild animals and plants to make houses, roads, factories and farms.

WHAT YOU CAN DO

You can help wild animals by giving them a place to live.
Make a wildlife park in your back garden! Small animals will be happy to come and live there.

A WILDLIFE PARK!

To start your wildlife park, find a patch of ground which nobody uses. Perhaps there's a bit at the bottom of your garden. Clear away any rubbish that's on it. Take a look at your soil. Is it light or dark, sticky or crumbly, moist or dry?

There are lots of different types of soil. The way it looks and feels depends on what's in it.

WHAT SOIL IS MADE OF

SAND: Sand is just rock which has been broken down into fine grains over millions of years.

CLAY: Clay is rock which has become a fine powder. It feels like a smooth paste when mixed with water.

WATER: This is needed by plants and animals.

HUMUS: This is the rotting remains of dead plants and animals. Humus provides food for plants which grow in the soil.

AIR: The gaps between bits of soil are full of air. Tiny creatures that live in the soil breathe this air.

DEBRIS: You may also find bits of broken pottery, stones, bricks, bones, bottle tops, coins and so on.

Cacti can live in dry sandy soil

The Red Campion likes damp soil with lots of humus in it

Different types of plant like different types of soil. No matter what type of soil you have, some plants will come and grow there. So will tiny creatures...

MEET THE MICROBES

The smallest living things are called microbes. They are too small to see without a powerful microscope. Many of them live in the soil.

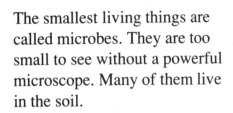

CUP OF SOIL FACT
One cup of soil may contain more living creatures than there are people in the whole world!

ALGAE
Sometimes you can see green patches of algae on damp rocks and on the surface of the soil.

Bacteria are very small.
Imagine that a single bacterium could grow to the size of this full stop.
Then it would be three hundred times its normal size.
An average human being growing by this much would be half a kilometre tall.

FUNGI
Mushrooms and toadstools are fungi. Many other types are too small to see. Fungi live on other plants and on animals.

BACTERIA
These are tiny plants. When plants and animals die, they are eaten by bacteria. This is what is happening when dead things rot away.

PROTOZOA
These are the smallest animals. They eat some bacteria and other types of bacteria eat them!

MITES AND WORMS

You may be able to see some tiny creatures without a microscope. Here are just a few of them...

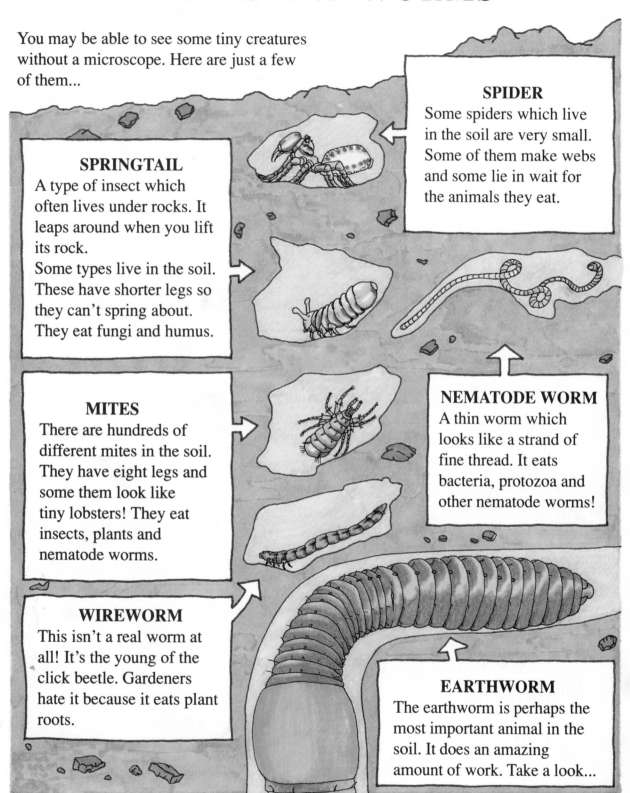

SPIDER
Some spiders which live in the soil are very small. Some of them make webs and some lie in wait for the animals they eat.

SPRINGTAIL
A type of insect which often lives under rocks. It leaps around when you lift its rock.
Some types live in the soil. These have shorter legs so they can't spring about. They eat fungi and humus.

MITES
There are hundreds of different mites in the soil. They have eight legs and some them look like tiny lobsters! They eat insects, plants and nematode worms.

NEMATODE WORM
A thin worm which looks like a strand of fine thread. It eats bacteria, protozoa and other nematode worms!

WIREWORM
This isn't a real worm at all! It's the young of the click beetle. Gardeners hate it because it eats plant roots.

EARTHWORM
The earthworm is perhaps the most important animal in the soil. It does an amazing amount of work. Take a look...

WORMS

Worms do more to make
soil than any other creature.

THE EXCITING LIFE OF AN EARTH WORM

Worms are male and female at the
same time. But...two worms need to get
together to mate.

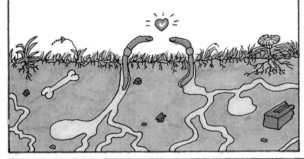

After mating, each worm lays its eggs.
Each worm then makes a slimy nest
where the eggs hatch into new worms.

Worms don't lay eggs every day. Mostly
they dig tunnels and eat a lot.

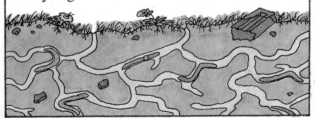

Some birds can pick worms out of the
soil. Worms usually stay out of reach
during the day.

WORM HAIR TEST

A worm has lots of tiny hairs on its skin.
These help it to grip the soil.

Remember
to put me
back in
the soil!

Gently pick up a worm. Put it in a glass
bowl. It won't be able to climb the sides
because its hairs can't grip the shiny glass.

Worms often climb to the surface at
night. They usually leave their tails in
their wormholes so that they can
quickly escape from danger.

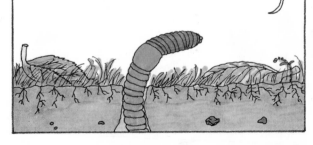

WORMS

The earthworm reaches out of its hole and pulls a leaf down from the surface.

The worm drags the leaf underground where it's safe to eat it. Some big worms go down as far as three metres from the surface.

Worms also have to eat soil to make their tunnels. They digest the little bits of plant material in the soil and pass the rest out behind them.

Some worms leave their droppings on the surface. These droppings are often soil from deep down. They are called worm casts.

EARTHWORM EARTH FACT

20 tonnes of soil

All the worms in a grass field the size of a football pitch can move a lorry-load of soil in a year.

That means that worms turn the soil. They move deep soil to the surface and drag leaves underground. This helps to bring humus into the deep soil.

Worm tunnels help air and water to reach the roots of plants. This also helps the other soil creatures which need air and water.

SPRING AND SEEDS

When Spring comes, plants will grow in your wildlife park. Many plants grow from seeds. Some grow from pieces of root in the soil. Most seeds fall in Autumn and stay in the soil until Spring. Here are a few different types of seeds.

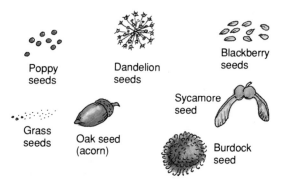

Poppy seeds

Dandelion seeds

Blackberry seeds

Grass seeds

Oak seed (acorn)

Sycamore seed

Burdock seed

HOW SEEDS ARRIVE IN YOUR WILDLIFE PARK

Birds called jays often bury acorns to eat later on. They sometimes forget where they've buried them. Then an oak tree can grow from the acorn.

Some seeds are so small you can hardly see them. Grass seeds in the air can cause hay fever.

Some seeds, such as sycamore and dandelion seeds, are blown by the wind.

Birds can't digest the seeds from some berries. So bird droppings sometimes contain blackberry seeds for example.

Some seeds have hooks, which stick to animals as they brush past the plants. Then the seeds fall off the animal's fur and drop onto the soil. The burdock plant has seeds like this.

Seeds from nearby plants can fall into tiny cracks and holes in the soil.

Why not add some wildflower seeds of your own? A mixture of plants will be good for your wildlife park.

PLANTING WILDFLOWERS

It's not easy to find seeds by yourself.

And...there wouldn't be any wildflowers left in the countryside if everybody picked them. Some plants are protected by law.

So...it's best to buy packets of wildflower seeds from a garden centre. Try to get lots of different sorts of seeds in case some won't grow in your soil.

HOW TO PLANT WILDFLOWER SEEDS

Make a hole in the soil about 2 cms deep.	Drop a seed in the hole.	Cover the hole with soil and press down gently.

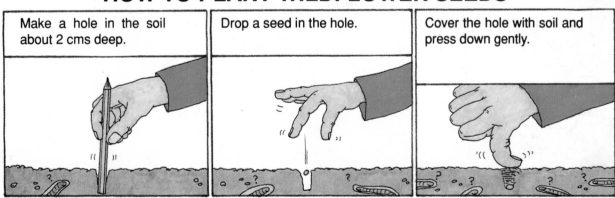

Many wildflowers and weeds are quite tough. But you may need to water them when they're still small. Water them if the soil gets very dry.

FARMS AND HEDGES

Nowadays there are fewer and fewer wildflowers in the countryside. This is partly because farmers are ploughing up more and more land to grow food crops. They're also pulling up hedges to make bigger fields. Many wildflowers and animals live in hedges and meadows.

In Britain, farmers have removed 225,000 kilometres of hedges since 1969. That's enough to stretch six times round the world! Your wildlife park will give plants and animals a small place to live.

Your seeds will grow in your wildlife park as long as there's some rain and sunlight.

But...you'll have to be patient. Your plants won't grow as quickly as you'd like!..

WEEDKILLERS

Some gardeners add strong poisons to the soil. These kill plants that the gardeners don't want.

BUT...some of these weedkillers are so strong that nothing will grow after the soil has been poisoned. Small animals which feed on the plants are also killed.

AND...sometimes weedkillers used on plants are washed into the rivers and into our drinking water.
SO...make your wildlife park a WEEDKILLER-FREE ZONE!

POISON FACT

A tiny dose of the weedkiller called paraquat can kill you. Weedkillers can be dangerous for people as well as plants!

It's a good idea to grow lots of different plants in your wildlife park. They will become food for many kinds of animals, especially insects...

11

INSECT INSPECTION

There are more than seven hundred thousand different types of insect. That's more than all the other types of animal put together! You can be sure that lots of insects will come and live in your wildlife park.

Inspect your soil and plants. Here are some of the insects you may see...

SPIDER FACT

SPIDER   **INSECT**

Spiders aren't insects. Insects have six legs and spiders have eight. Most insects have wings and spiders don't. Most spiders eat insects, but some insects, such as the spider wasp, hunt for spiders!

GREENFLY

These live by sucking sap from the stems and leaves of plants. Gardeners don't like greenfly because they weaken plants. Greenfly droppings are a sort of sweet, sticky stuff which ants love. If you stand under an oak tree in Summer, you'll get covered in tiny droplets of this fluid which is called honey dew.

ANT

An ants' nest is a very well organised home built in several layers...a bit like an office block! One nest can contain thousands of ants.

BEE

Bees live in nests up trees or in beekeepers' hives. They make honey from the nectar in flowers. Honey-bees won't sting you unless you frighten them.

EARWIG

Earwigs look fierce but they can't bite with their pincers. Earwigs like to rest in a hole during the day. But don't worry, they won't crawl into your ear hole!

MALE   **FEMALE**

COLORADO BEETLE

Bright colours on insects often means they are poisonous or taste nasty to other creatures. The colorado beetle eats potato crops, so its main enemies are farmers.

BOMBADIER BEETLE

This beetle defends itself from enemies by squirting out a liquid which explodes in the air!

WASP BEETLE

This beetle lives on honey from flowers. It's protected from enemies by looking like a dangerous wasp.

STICK INSECT

Eats evergreen leaves such as ivy and privet. It keeps so still during the day that it looks like a dry twig. This saves it from being eaten by other animals.

MAGPIE MOTH

Antennae

Columbine flower

It's hard to tell the difference between moths and butterflies. Moths usually have fatter bodies and fly at night. Butterflies have little lumps on the end of their antennae and fly during the day.

GREEN-VEINED WHITE BUTTERFLY

Many plants need insects to help them to produce seeds. The way insects help is called pollination. It works like this...

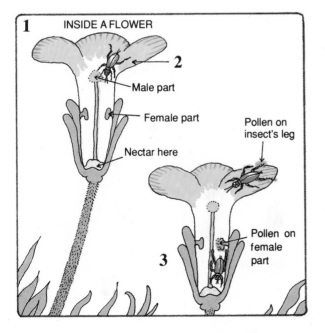

1   INSIDE A FLOWER
2
Male part
Female part
Nectar here
Pollen on insect's leg
Pollen on female part
3

1. Most flowers contain male and female parts and a sweet liquid called nectar. Insects like nectar.

2. To get to the nectar they have to squeeze past the male part of the flower. The insect rubs a fine dust called pollen from the male part.

3. The insect then visits another flower. The male pollen falls from the insect onto the female part of the flower. This fertilizes the flower so that a seed can be formed. Different flowers attract different creatures for pollination. For example, the aspidistra plant is pollinated by snails!

SLUGS AND SNAILS

As your plants grow bigger, larger animals will come to feed on them. Keep a look out for slugs and snails. They belong to the same family of animals as octopuses!..

SNAIL WATCH

1. Pick up a snail very gently.

2. Place it in a glass bowl.

3. Watch the snail from underneath and see how it moves.

4. Be sure to put the snail back where you found it...and to clean the bowl!

SNAIL TONGUE FACT

Snails have rough tongues, so if you're quiet, you can sometimes hear them eating!

People can eat some kinds of snails. BUT...the sort you find in the garden aren't the ones you can eat!

Some birds like to eat garden snails. If you keep still, you may see a blackbird cracking one open!

SLUGS AND SNAILS

A snail's shell helps to stop the snail from drying out. Slugs are like snails without shells. They need to keep their skin damp, so they are covered in a sticky slime. Slugs taste nasty and so most birds won't eat them.

Gardeners don't like slugs and snails which eat garden plants. To kill slugs, gardeners sometimes put poisonous slug pellets on the soil. When a slug eats one of these pellets, its body dries up and it dies.

SLUG DUNG FACT

Some slug experts say that slug droppings help the microbes which eat dead leaves.

Animals often eat our plants. But we shouldn't try to kill them with chemicals. Slug pellets can kill other animals as well.
A bird which eats a poisoned snail will be poisoned too!

FLIES

Most small animals have lots of young. Some flies lay up to three thousand eggs at a time!

Imagine...

...a fly lays three thousand eggs in April...

...and they all hatch out. If each female lays another three thousand eggs...

Eggs turn into maggots

Maggots turn into flies

...and so on...

...by August the whole world would be covered with a layer of flies fourteen metres deep!

But don't worry. This doesn't happen because...
1. There just isn't enough food for that many flies!
2. Other animals come along and eat the eggs and the flies.

Animals which eat other animals are called predators. Almost everything can be a meal for another creature...

LADYBIRDS
eat
GREENFLY

BLACKBIRDS
eat
SNAILS

SPIDERS
eat
INSECTS

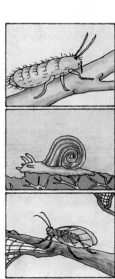

PESTS

Some animals like to eat our food crops. Farmers grow huge fields full of potatoes, wheat, cabbages and so on. This encourages large numbers of animals to move in and eat their favourite foods.

The caterpillars of some butterflies like eating cabbages.

Predators move in to eat the caterpillars.

Phew! I'm full!

Gardeners and farmers call crop-eating animals pests. When there's plenty of food to eat, the pests produce lots of young.

Then there are too many pests and the predators can't eat them all.

Many farmers and gardeners spray their plants with pesticides. These are chemicals which kill pests.

BUT....many pesticides kill the predators too!

GREENFLY PEST FACT

A gardener once counted 24,688 greenfly on a single tomato plant!

SO...it's best not to use pesticides, especially in the garden. Your wildlife park can be a home for ladybirds and greenfly too!

All sorts of other animals will come and live in your wildlife park if you grow enough different plants.

HABITATS

All living things need food, water and a place to live. The area that an animal lives in is called its habitat.

Each kind of animal likes to live in its own sort of habitat. Your wildlife park will provide lots of different habitats for small animals.

IN HEDGES
Look carefully at a hedge. You'll see hundreds of garden spiders and their webs. Because they're high up, they can catch flying insects.

IN WOOD
Look for tiny, round holes in wooden fences. Young woodworm eat the wood until they've grown enough to leave. Then they fly out of the holes they've made.

ON PLANTS
Gardeners hate nettles but many butterflies love them. They live on nectar from the flowers. Caterpillars live on the leaves.

UNDER FALLEN LEAVES
Woodlice eat the rotting wood and fallen leaves which they live in. They can also hide there from predators.

UNDER GROUND
The soil provides a dark, damp place to live for thousands of different creatures.

UNDER ROCKS AND BRICKS
Creatures such as millipedes and centipedes hide under stones. They usually eat dead leaves.

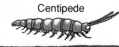
Centipede

Millipede

SUMMER HABITATS

Here's something you can do in Summer when there's lots of animals looking for a home. Collect a few small piles of garden rubbish and other old items. Put them on the edge of your wildlife park.

A PILE OF LEAVES

A PILE OF STICKS

SOME BROKEN BRICKS

AN OLD BUCKET

A BROKEN TOY

AN OLD SHIRT

Leave these home-made habitats for two weeks. Then carefully take a look at the animals which have moved in.
Don't try wearing the shirt though!..

HOW ABOUT A GARDEN POND?

A garden pond will be a habitat for lots of animals. It's best to start your wildlife pond in early Summer.

Dig a hole in the ground.

Put an old washing-up bowl in it.

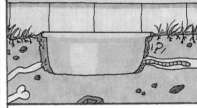

Pack soil up to the rim of the bowl, so there's no gap.

Ask your mum or dad to help you to collect some mud and water. You'll find some at the bottom of a pond or ditch.

Pour the water and mud into your pond. Then lean a stick up the side. Animals which fall in can climb up it...so they don't drown!

Now sit back and wait. Your pond is already full of life. The mud at the bottom holds millions of tiny plants and animals. When they've grown bigger, you'll be able to see them.

After three weeks, dip a jam jar in the water, then look closely.

You could see some amazing animals!

POND PANORAMA

Here are just a few of the animals you could find in your pond...

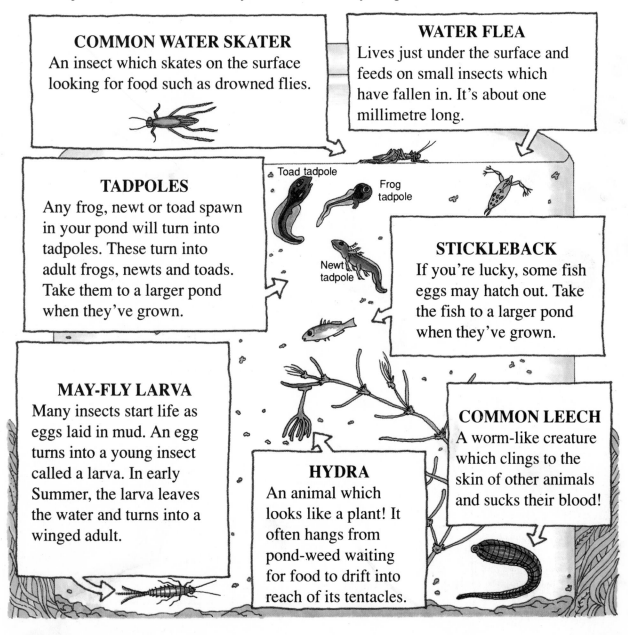

COMMON WATER SKATER
An insect which skates on the surface looking for food such as drowned flies.

WATER FLEA
Lives just under the surface and feeds on small insects which have fallen in. It's about one millimetre long.

TADPOLES
Any frog, newt or toad spawn in your pond will turn into tadpoles. These turn into adult frogs, newts and toads. Take them to a larger pond when they've grown.

Toad tadpole

Frog tadpole

Newt tadpole

STICKLEBACK
If you're lucky, some fish eggs may hatch out. Take the fish to a larger pond when they've grown.

MAY-FLY LARVA
Many insects start life as eggs laid in mud. An egg turns into a young insect called a larva. In early Summer, the larva leaves the water and turns into a winged adult.

HYDRA
An animal which looks like a plant! It often hangs from pond-weed waiting for food to drift into reach of its tentacles.

COMMON LEECH
A worm-like creature which clings to the skin of other animals and sucks their blood!

Most ponds are fed by streams or rainwater. You'll need to keep your smaller pond topped up with tap water, especially in Summer.

If you want larger pond animals to come and live in your wildlife park, ask your parents to build a garden pond.

TOADS

If you're lucky, a toad may move
into your wildlife park.
Toads are fun. You can teach them to
take food from your hand!..

Make a home for your toad.
Put some grass and leaves inside an
old cocoa tin. A toad will like this
home-made home!

TOAD EYEBALL FACT

Toads chew their food, such as worms,
with their eyeball muscles. That's why
they close their eyes when they're eating!

OLD TOAD FACT

Your toad could still be around when
you've grown up. Toads live for up
to forty years!

FAT TOAD FACT

Toads can puff themselves up with
air when they're frightened by
predators. This makes animals such
as snakes think they're too big to eat!

TOAD PIMPLE FACT

The lumps on a toad's skin contain a
slime which tastes nasty. This often
saves toads from being eaten by birds!

WHAT EATS WHAT?

Animals live by eating plants or each other.

Check what you've found out so far...

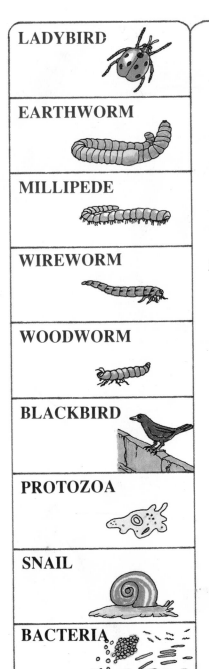

LADYBIRD

EARTHWORM

MILLIPEDE

WIREWORM

WOODWORM

BLACKBIRD

PROTOZOA

SNAIL

BACTERIA

Which of the creatures on the left eat which of the creatures on the right? You'll find the answers upside-down below!

ANSWERS:

Bacteria eat almost anything

Snails eat fresh leaves and dead leaves

Protozoa eat bacteria

Blackbirds eat earthworms and snails

Woodworm eat wood

Wireworms eat plant roots

Millipedes eat dead leaves

Earthworms eat bacteria and dead leaves

Ladybirds eat greenfly

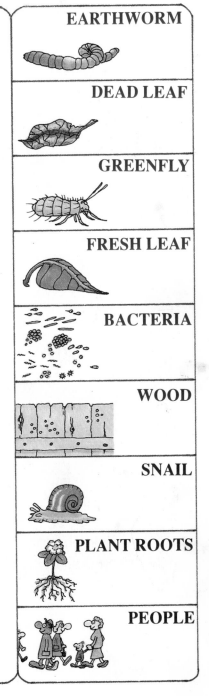

EARTHWORM

DEAD LEAF

GREENFLY

FRESH LEAF

BACTERIA

WOOD

SNAIL

PLANT ROOTS

PEOPLE

MAKING NOTES

You can find out about small animals by studying them closely.

But...some animals are too small for you to see properly. A magnifying glass will help you to see them better.

You can buy a good one from a toy shop. Get a notebook too, and set out half of the pages like this...

DATE	TIME	ANIMALS	WHERE SEEN	COMMENTS
APRIL 2	10.30 am	Woodlice	Under leaves	Lots of them
APRIL 2	11.00 am	Toad	under a hedge	Looked sleepy
APRIL 3	10.00 am	Centipede	under a stone	20 pairs of legs
APRIL 3	10.40 am	Boy next door	Treading on my plants	FAT HEAD!

Use the other pages to draw the animals you see. You may be lucky and spot some creatures that nobody's ever seen before. New animals are being discovered all the time. You might not be able to find out the names of the animals you've seen. Draw them anyway, and make up your own names for them!

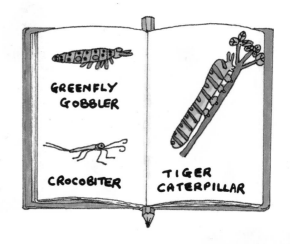

GREENFLY GOBBLER

CROCOBITER

TIGER CATERPILLAR

HANDLING SMALL ANIMALS

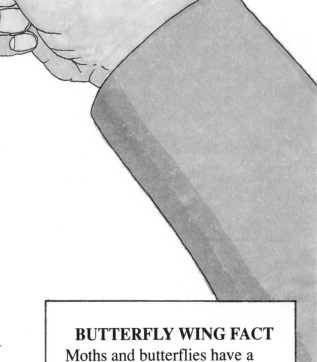

Imagine what it would be like to be picked up by a great big hand from the sky!

If you need to pick up an animal to study it, do it gently.

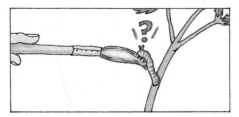

1. Pick up very small creatures with a leaf, spoon or paintbrush.

EEK!

2. Don't put them in small matchboxes or tins.

3. Only study them for a short while. Then return them to where you found them.

BUTTERFLY WING FACT
Moths and butterflies have a fine powder on their wings which helps them to fly. Never pick up butterflies by the wings. You may damage them.

SHREWS, VOLES AND MICE

Some animals produce milk for their young. These kinds of animals are called mammals.
Human beings are mammals.
So are shrews, voles and mice.

Small mammals such as these make paths between the stems of plants. This keeps them partly hidden from flying predators. You must keep very still and quiet if you want to see them. They might visit your wildlife park from a nearby hedge.

COMMON SHREW
Eats up to three times its own weight in insects every day!

PIGMY SHREW
An insect eater. A very busy animal. It uses up its energy so quickly, it has to eat almost all the time to stay alive!

FIELD VOLE
Eats insects and some plants. Voles store food underground to eat in Winter.

WOODMOUSE
Loves strawberries. Has very poor eyesight. You can get very close to one if you creep up quietly.

FAT CATS

Shrews, voles and mice can be food for larger animals such as owls and stoats. Nowadays, small animals in gardens are more likely to be killed by cats. There are a lot more cats than owls or stoats.

Your cuddly pussycat could be more than it seems.

When you're not watching, it could be a dangerous killer!

FAT CAT FACT

Wildlife experts say that British cats kill more than one hundred million small animals and birds each year. Cats don't need to kill for food because their owners feed them.

Cats used to be wild creatures which hunted for food before they learnt to live in people's houses. Most cats can't help hunting small animals. It's no use trying to stop them.

Just one cat in your street will not kill too many animals. The problem is that such a lot of houses have cats. So...don't forget the damage to wildlife if you're thinking of getting a kitten.

Cats will chase almost any small, moving thing!

AUTUMN

Late Summer and Autumn is the time when most trees and plants die down. Their leaves form a layer of leaf litter on the ground.

This leaf litter makes a new habitat for millions of animals and bacteria. Here are just three of them...

LEAF SKELETON FACT

Oak leaf

Sometimes you can see leaves like this. Lots of insects such as caterpillars eat leaves. The veins of the leaves are hard to chew, so they aren't always eaten... leaving a leaf skeleton!

BRANDLING WORM
Eats leaves and rotting fruit. Helps to turn dead plants into new soil.

HARVESTMAN
A spider which hunts amongst leaves for insects. It doesn't spin a web.

BRISTLETAIL
Eats rotting plants.

Before Autumn is over, many dead plants have been eaten and turned into animal droppings.

The droppings and the remains of dead animals become mixed with dust to make new soil.

'DUST GETS EVERYWHERE' FACT

Some of the dust which settles in Europe is blown from the Sahara Desert in Africa!

AUTUMN

Autumn is also the time when there are lots of seeds, berries and nuts to eat. Because there is so much food, this is the time when you'll find the most animals in your wildlife park.
Look out for wasps eating rotting fruit.

Are there any large trees nearby? If so, seeds and nuts may fall into your garden. You may be lucky and see a squirrel on a nut hunt!

Walnut

SANTA CLAWS

But... by late Autumn, the plants are dying away and the food is running out.
Animals have to start preparing for Winter.

WHAT ANIMALS DO IN WINTER

STAY IN EGG OR CHRYSALIS

Most adult insects die, but many young insects stay in eggs or in a chrysalis until Spring.

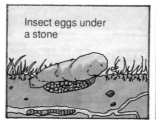
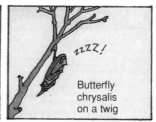

MIGRATE

Birds which eat insects in Summer have to fly away to a warmer country to find food in Winter.

HIBERNATE

This is like a long, deep sleep. Animals don't need to eat when they're asleep. That means they don't have to go out to look for food so often. The dormouse sleeps about six months of the year!

DIE OF COLD

Small animals die of cold very easily. Many mammals grow extra fur for warmth. Some birds huddle in large groups to stay warm.

GET EATEN

DIE OF HUNGER

It's hard for animals to find food when the soil is covered with snow and frost. Worms tunnel deep down below the frozen part of the soil.

WHAT YOU CAN DO IN WINTER

Only the strongest animals live through the Winter. Birds will visit your wildlife park all year round. But when Winter comes, they won't find so much to eat. You can help some of them to survive by putting food out for them.
Why not make a bird table?

WHAT TO DO...

FOOD FOR BIRDS

BREAD   BACON RIND

SEEDS   CAKE   FAT

BISCUITS   CHEESE

And you can give birds a bowl of warm water on frosty days.

Nail an old wooden tray or a flat piece of wood to a tall post. Put food on it every day.

Birds will get used to seeing food on their table. If there's no food, some birds will wait too long for it and will die of cold. So...don't forget to keep on feeding the birds.

Put the bird table high enough to be out of reach of cats.

Some birds will only eat food on the ground. Remember to scatter some food there too.

Now sit back and wait for Spring to begin all over again. Next year, your wildlife park will have more life in it than ever!..

31

Every year, the small creatures, and especially the worms, will help your wildlife park to grow.
More and more plants and animals will move in.
Then you can invite your friends on wildlife safaris!

BUT DON'T GET LOST
IN THE JUNGLE!

INDEX

Air 3, 7
Algae 4
Ant 12
Aspidistra 13
Autumn 28, 29
Bacteria 4, 5, 28
Bee 12
Beekeepers 12
Birds 6-8, 14, 15, 22, 30, 31
Bird table 31
Blackbird 14, 16
Bombardier Beetle 13
Brandling Worm 28
Bristletail 28
Butterfly 13, 25, 30
Cacti 3
Caterpillar 17,18,25
Cats 27
Centipede 18
Chrysalis 30
Clay 3
Colorado Beetle 13
Common Shrew 26
Common Water Skater 21
Crops 10, 13, 17
Debris 3
Dormouse 30
Droppings 8, 12, 15, 28
Dust 28
Earthworm 5-7
Earwig 12
Eggs 6, 16, 30
Farmers 10, 13, 17
Field Vole 26
Flies 16
Frog 21

Fungi 4, 5
Garden centres 9
Gardeners 11, 15, 18
Garden pond 20, 21
Greenfly 12, 16, 17
Green-veined White Butterfly 13
Habitats 18-20, 22
Handling small animals 25
Harvestman 28
Hedges 10, 18
Hibernation 30
Honey 12, 13
Humus 3, 5
Hydra 21
Insects 5, 11-13, 16, 18, 26, 30
Jay 8
Ladybird 15-17
Leaves 7, 13, 18, 19, 22, 28
Magpie Moth 13
Mammals 26, 30
May Fly larva 21
Meadows 10
Migration 30
Millipede 18
Mites 5
Nectar 12
Nematode worm 5
Newt 21
Notebook 24
Nuts 29
Oak tree 8, 12
Owl 27
Pesticides 17
Pests 17

Pigmy Shrew 26
Pollination 13
Predators 16, 17, 22, 26
Protozoa 4, 5
Red Campion 3
Sand 3
Seeds 8, 29
Slug 14, 15
Slug pellets 15
Snail 13-16
Snake 22
Soil 3-9, 28, 30
Spiders 5, 12, 16, 18, 28
Spring 8
Springtails 5
Squirrel 29
Stick Insect 13
Stickleback 21
Stoat 27
Summer 19
Tadpoles 21
Toad 22
Uncle Octopus 14
Wasp 13, 29
Wasp Beetle 13
Water 3, 7, 9-11, 20, 21, 31
Water Flea 21
Weedkillers 11
Wildflowers 8, 9, 10
Wildlife safari 32
Winter 29-31
Wireworm 5
Woodlouse 8
Woodmouse 26
Woodworm 8, 18
Worm casts 7
Worms 1, 5-7, 30